LARVAE *of the* NEAREST STARS

LARVAE
of the
NEAREST
STARS

Poems

Catherine W. Carter

Louisiana State University Press   Baton Rouge

Published with the assistance of the Sea Cliff Fund

Published by Louisiana State University Press
Copyright © 2019 by Catherine Carter
All rights reserved
Manufactured in the United States of America
LSU Press Paperback Original
FIRST PRINTING

DESIGNER: Mandy McDonald Scallan
TYPEFACE: Whitman
PRINTER AND BINDER: LSI

Library of Congress Cataloging-in-Publication Data
Names: Carter, Catherine, 1967– author.
Title: Larvae of the nearest stars : poems / Catherine Carter.
Description: Baton Rouge : Louisiana State University Press, [2019]
Identifiers: LCCN 2019008227| ISBN 978-0-8071-6988-9 (pbk. : alk. paper) | ISBN
    978-0-8071-7231-5 (pdf) | ISBN 9780807172322 (epub)
Classification: LCC PS3603.A7769 A6 2019 | DDC 811/.6—dc23

Grateful acknowledgment is made to the editors and staffs of the following publica-
tions, in which the poems listed appeared previously, sometimes in slightly different
form: *About Place:* "After the Colony Collapse, Cullowhee, North Carolina"; *Asheville
Poetry Review:* "The Young" and "First Witch"; *Barefoot Muse:* "The Globe"; *Cold
Mountain Review:* "The Rapture"; *Cortland Review:* "Ways to Talk about Decay";
Delmarva Review: "Snail Kite"; *Ecotone:* "Hornets' Nest"; *Flying South:* "Disaster,
Walking" and "April, 1978"; *Kakalak:* "The Lycanthrope"; *Mississippi Review:* "The
Things You Know"; *North Carolina Literary Review:* "Billy Collins Pours Me a Beer"
and "Womb-room"; *Pinesong:* "Day of the Dead"; *Poetry in Plain Sight:* "Squash
Vine" and "Luna"; *Right Hand Pointing:* "First Signs"; *Southern Humanities Review:*
"Lactobacilli"; *Southern Poetry Anthology:* "Two-Seater"; *South Writ Large:* "Ghost
Season"; *Still, the Journal:* "Wooly Adelgid," "Chickweed, Hens," "Night Driving,
Lighted Windows," and "The Promise"; *Tar River Poetry:* "Walking Home at Night,
with Sonda" and "After Anguish"; *Whale Road Review,* "Hot Flash."

Grateful acknowledgment is also made to Richard Krawiec and Jacar Press for pub-
lication of the chapbook *Marks of the Witch* (winter 2014), in which the following
poems first appeared, sometimes in slightly different versions: "Fairy Tale," "Mortal
Minerals," "River of Anguish," "The Things You Know," "What's Eating You," "What I
Came Back For," "Volta," and "The Wheel."

For Tom Horton,
  and in memory of Kathryn Stripling Byer:
who fit watersheds and mountains
    into spaces the size of a book

CONTENTS

LARVAE *of the* NEAREST STARS

Fernshadow Creek

Back then all the cars had faces. Some trees did too.
And the little spillway you craned to see
as the schoolbus ground past, bearing you into bond,
you gave that a secret name, you thought
it housed a spirit. You gave everything names.

Freeway lights were pinned angels,
inhumanly tall, stub heads, stretching their arm-wings
and splayed hands as far as they could to hold
transparent jewels of light, stuck there forever. Who
would do this to angels you never asked;
you knew no one could tell.

And the ground was royal, for the rain
decked it with spiky crowns, praised it with clear flowers.
How were you to know?

The stoplights were long yellow faces.
Red, they glared with one stern, sore eye,
glad to say NO. Then they opened round mouths
in a long green howl of some unknowable woe: *go, go.*

So you went along, never knew if your world
was the world, who saw what you saw—
if they did, no one could tell—
turned deaf to the stoplight's wail.
And yet that world comes back,
the world where you find yourself at forty,
or fifty, crouched by a stream named
for some man, watching the skeletal marks
the arched fronds of Christmas
ferns throw on its trembleglass, and before
you know it, you speak out of your own
round mouth, giving it a secret

name. *Fernshadow Creek,* you say,
praising it with clear crowns and words as if
you were young again, seeing it again
out of your own sore eyes, telling
what no one else can tell.

Ghost Season

Shed leaves are everywhere, numerous as souls
of the dead. They tumble and plunge in the cold
shallow river, hurrying
on to the black deeps of the dammed
lake at the end. Some ride
the surface tension, still
grasping at their element, air;
some have begun to sink,
caught in the transparent
currents tugging below the brim-skin.
Others go dry, crisped as if
with fire; they mass in the road,
huddle under logs, unsure where
they're supposed to go—the instructions
were unclear. And they come, as if led,
to the portals of this house: some wedged
in crevice and cornice, some driven
between screens. Some dash in like cats
when I open a door, crumbly but
stealthy, hoping perhaps
for a place they can stay. They
rustle like ghosts, voices mostly
gone. An oak leaf long
as my forearm, tobacco-brown,
eddies down a clear spiral of air,
floats through the door I hold ajar:
inconsequent, nonchalant, *nobody
here but us leaves.* I pin it with a stare,
lift it by the stem. *Grandpa?* I say.
Grandmother? Isabel? Which one are you?

Ancestors, Names

Porters opened doors vast enough to be
a full-time job, Cartwrights trued wheels and honed
spokes, Wards strove not to offend the family.
Masons slapped bricks into wet mortar, Smiths
battered molten iron, MacSomethings and
O'Somethings were children of their fathers—their
kindred their identities. Westbrooks
lived by some westward stream, and of course
Carters pushed or pulled or drove on endless
dusty world-girdling roads: curled terrible whips
in the cringing air, cursed recalcitrant
oxen and sheared lynch-pins, plunged despairing
into ruts axle-break deep, somehow dragged
their wagons out. But what lay behind
the doors the porters opened up—feasts of
stag, god-kings, women of iron—or why
the wards stayed so long, or who got bricked up
behind the masons' best work, who knows? Or
what my humble forebears carted. Some, to
be sure, we can guess—sacks of barley, tuns
of wine, bushels of purple turnips, blood-
smudged crossbow quarrels. But more, too: the light-
riding ghosts of their dear dead, the heavy-
jolting corpses of plague. Famine-bread baked
invisibly with ergot. Some mewling
baby familiar for the local witch.
And have the times changed, aren't we still tugging
at doors, seeking families not our own,
sanding axles to the roll of history,
hauling around the dead? and this handcart
rattles heavy with books, quarrels, ghosts, bread
that may bring strange visions, or not. It's light
compared to most; still, it galls at shoulder

and thigh. Another step, another: I'll
drag this cart through, if I can, I'll pull this
load as far as I can. Here come pitted
wheel-ruts, gleaming bright with acid rain. How
deep? Any way around? None I can see.

The Drought

It hadn't gotten this dry where she came from:
this was before warming went global, though even then
some summers lasted till only deluge would do
to lay the swirling drought-devils low.
But this was different, this was worse.
What he was when they met, even she didn't know
by the time he came home from his war
grim and drunk. What he saw there, he never
said. If once they'd teased or joked together,
forgiven each other for being who they were,
that was long over; by then nobody knew it.
What showed were the grooves in his face like sores,
deep as tire ruts months after the last rain-trace
has evanesced, and from her, the raised hairbrush trembling
with endurance, enforced forbearance. Would enough
love have saved either of them? Who knows,
what's enough. And few of us forgive anyone
anyway for changing, or for staying the same.
She wouldn't've believed, before, how easy it was to stop
trying; back then, maybe she would've said
what women did: *you're supposed to stand*
by him, you have to get through it,
that gouge of will. But things got drier.
His tongue shrank with thirst;
she broke his glass canteens; the fires
began. It would've taken another flood
to soften the cracked mud of her long rage
against his angry misery, and was she God
to call water out of that glaring sky?
She wasn't, and she couldn't do it.

Where I Stand

Each day I stand up before classrooms,
and though not very tall, I tower
over the young, the ill-read, command
those rooms from the height of all
that's under my feet.
I was heaved up here on the shoulders
of the educated, who educated
me—songs, books, checks—
who were taught because
others taught them, because back
along the chain was enough
food, enough leisure to build love
for books and silver, songs and land:
enough in part because in their turn
some under my feet balance on the hard
foundation of the big Virginia house, the one
still standing over its cotton and corn
and bones. Up here, tall
as a poplar in rich dirt,
pale as oak, I teach
from the top of this trembling heap
of the dead and the not yet
dead: scarred backs, sold
children, lost languages
and names, those other
chains. When I turn
to go, I must pick my way with care—
they are so uneasy
in their perilous balance, so slick
with the vomit and the tears, the pus
and the blood, the soft shudder of pulse.

Disaster, Walking

I am come like time, the waster of peoples,
like death, the destroyer of worlds.
Where the marsh shelters a rare sea aster,
there I trip, stagger, and crush. Where
a sprinkler head lurks in long grass,
there my blind heel falls, smashing
and shattering. If the lid of a jar
in the cupboard is loose, that jar I seize,
and the ensuing crash, the splash
of vinegar and glass, are vast.
These feet are drawn to slicks of algae,
plasters of mud, these shins to sharp corners,
these fingers to burners that blister
and ratchets that bruise; I bite
my own cheeks, poke my own eyes.
The sleeve of my T-shirt snags the toilet
paper holder, yanks it right out of the wall.
If I tug on a shade, it unfurls forever. Never
master of my hands, avatar of chaos
and entropy, I stumble across the earth's crust,
slipping, dropping, doing
damage, sometimes slow, sometimes fast
as a javelin hurled by some three-eyed god
of not-so-random. At last even my mother said
you are a walking disaster,
and who should know better than she,
who opened the gates of flesh to free me,
who loosed me upon this world?

First Witch

A water witch, they called him: a dowser,
summoned to conjure water up from sand
on which a steel windmill might soon stand
to draw that water out to feed peppers
and tomatoes, pussy willows and beans.
He had a wand, but not a special one:
any split stick would do. *But how*, we asked,
cutting our own forked sticks, trying our dry luck.
Maybe not even the witch knew how.
He called to water; water answered him.
After he found it, the dowser let me
set young, weak hands before his on the wand,
right there where I'd stood before, feeling not
one twitch or tremor, and there it was,
the pull toward the earth: magnet-strong, strong
as love, or the deeper wells I hadn't yet
slipped into and half-drowned. And the stick bent
and twisted under my hands: a promise
or warning of all the earthly magics
still to come, the currents that I'd never
find alone, the common stick's witch-works
illuminating unseen lines and forces
coursing, electric, arcane, through the whole
dark body of our mundane sandy world.

The Globe

We were quite small still when you brought the globe
home from wherever you found it, made of tin
and circumscribed by a white plastic stand,
but rolling smoothly as the real world
you must have thought that it would teach us of,
like the encyclopedias downstairs,
the dictionaries you taught us to read.
We liked to whirl it, set a tiny dog
on a magnetic strip on top of Russia
to slide along, pushed by the arch of frame
as the globe spun: counterclockwise, you said.
We liked the colors, bright in pink and green,
the names of places now no longer there,
Constantinople that's now Istanbul
again. I doubt that we learned much about
far places, or the way the world was made,
or that we ever thanked you for the globe
we might have asked you for, if we had thought;
you gave it to us anyway. And now
it's somewhat late to speak of all the things
you gave us anyway, those turquoise seas
between the gaily-colored continents,
plus things one can't ask any globe to show:
the path down through our green woods to the river
we called ours too, the words, the work, the world
you gave to us, all somehow crammed inside
the long uneven quadrant of the line-stones
(all but covered over now with earth)
that held, and hold, our first world's boundaries.

April, 1978

High in the whorled wheels of the white pine's
spoked branches, we could see two timelines.
One was the every-year stream that flowed
down there below, month following week,
the time in which our sweatshirt sleeves shrank
gradually shorter. But up here—
the grass-cool wind swinging the whole tree
in its shallow arc, the bark crusted
with seaglass lichen on its rough scales,
the air sharp with the silver-blue needles'
resin—up here was the other time,
our time: the one that we inhabited
not knowing that we did, or that not
everyone did. In pine-time our sleeves
would always reach our wrists, never-washed
jersey stay fresh. Up here, wouldn't it
always be this Saturday morning
in April, nineteen seventy-eight,
the same two vultures describing the
same two arcs like compasses, veering
only to wheel back? And though we knew
that soon enough we'd have to climb down
through twilight where dead branches sharpened
jags to punch right through jersey into
childflesh, we didn't remember then
that our pine's roots were in that other time,
or foresee its fall, or guess which year
(nineteen eighty-six): oh, no, not us,
our hands still sticky with the pungent sap
of everlasting morning, turning black.

Two-Seater

The shingle-roofed Crazy Acres outhouse
has two seats. Plain shack of pine
board, 1911, brick cellar, two seats.
Some had four; Rockefellers and Vanderbilts, six.
This world wasn't always the world
we know, purging bowels and spilling out
bladders in splendid isolation, pristine porcelain,
solitary cells. Sometimes, clearly,
people talked. Sisters sitting side
by side giggled over what no adult heard,
men handed over thin glossy
Sears leaves (wives adjuring them
not to use the page on Hats), boys compared
things. When the canning
jars bubbled death, or the pigs rooted too close
to the well, there was no wait at the door;
daughters held mothers' heads,
spouses who hated each other prayed
together to live, or to die, where they retched
up their hearts for a thread of slime,
and whether those words blunted the teeth
of the wind through the walls' broad cracks,
or the memory of kids dead of dysentery,
who knows? I don't.
I know that on Crazy Acres, two kids,
not so far back, did share those seats,
whispered and giggled there; they aren't dead
yet. I know last year a man ripped off
the rotting roof, stripped the ivy-gripped
walls, found the brick cellar
sound, and built it up again, two seats
and all, a crescent moon
on the door. I know this world
isn't always the world we know.

The Things You Know

You know the back way around Boyce Mill
for when the bridge is out at Gravelly Branch.
Your eyes still know the turn to Templeville
from the Smyrna road, even when it's blanched
by snow, and the sign down. Then there's a beech
grown spiral, in your neighbor's patch of woods,
you think you can still find, and there's the ditch
at the county line, where the first nematode
parasite you ever saw devoured a cricket
from inside. Your inner map's like that
a lot these days: *the viburnum thicket*
where two deer paused to stare, turn at
the log road just beside it—though that path
has faded till only your own can see it,
and though those deer have not drawn mortal breath
two decades now. But it works, albeit
up from beneath, obscurely; you'll still never
forget to watch your back in Big Elk Creek
for giant freighters ghosting from a river
that looks as slender as a garter snake.
And still there's so much more you could have learned
if you had stayed—you could have been the heir
to all the back roads, every creek your own—
if it weren't pointless now. If you lived there.

What's Eating You

The crickets always lurked in the floor,
but why you wake now to their slick
black eyes staring, those mandibles
clamped in your cheek, who knows.
Maybe the moon is wrong,
maybe it's just time. It's only
a tiny bite, but the cricket you fling
off with a shriek takes with it a bead
of you, a red fleck you won't get back.
The next night there are five. Then
comes the cone-nosed assassin bug,
proboscis built to sip blood. That isn't good;
but the toads are worse.
Those plates leave crescents, like the half-smiles
you give when people ask how you are. Then
the sparrows, you know
how that goes, those blunt-needle
beaks scissoring chunks like sunflower seeds,
and how the rats gouge steadier,
harder. The pecks and nips stay
small; if you died, who'd feed
them, commensals, obsessions,
pets who never tire of you? Night after
night they snatch their wet gobbets
and slink back. More of you
goes missing every day, and soon
you buy a nightlight; you might as well see.
It's never good, but good
is no match for familiar,
though you wear your familiar sleeves, fear
familiar eyes. Don't worry;
your secret is safe.
If anyone were going to notice
the scabs, the seeping

bites, this wouldn't happen.
The crickets, the rats, the clicking
of jaws in the wall—
they don't come to people who can tell,
they don't do this if anyone can see.

Distant Cousin, Jellyfish

Green with sungleam, the deep Atlantic swells
clasp you, feed you, rock you on their
backs, till suddenly they snarl and froth,
dash your head, rip your limbs, hurl
you up the anvil sand, suck themselves
away never to turn, or turn too late.
Crushed by your own weight,
you may die there—most do—in pain.
Or something may come and handle you.
That vertebrate might even mean you well,
as your heavy gold bell shrivels, the burning cells
on your silky filaments contract and dry;
touch may be mercy or death; you
can't tell. You're too soft
for anything but what you eat—
there's no touch even when you mate.
All contact is the same,
immediate, extreme:
every touch appalling when you're gel
with no bones, no skin, no shell.
All you have is a mouth, a bell.
If either had a tongue, you'd strike, you'd scream.

First Signs

Age, coming toward me in the summer
crowd, shouldered past, once,
then again. This time
she missed me
among the thousands, but where
her cool fingers brushed my arm, look,
these mottled spots, these tiny
bruises, brown as fallen prunes.

The High Road

Though the views are wide, the air is thin.
The way is strewn with stones, grown green
and lush with nettles, catbriar,
poison ivy, barred with dry piles
of fallen logs to clamber past,
scrape underneath. Trail maintenance,
not so much. Fellow hikers, not
so many. For company,
the silent vultures swinging higher
up, black wings glinting silver
dihedrals on the bright sky;
the occasional hovering,
quivering spark-blue dragonfly.

You know this path is the right one.
The other is for the dead and
those with vertigo in their souls.
You know the way you have to go.
And yet: those stones. Those roots and washed-
out gullies. Your own creeping weight.
The way so few know what you choose,
or care. Many despise the beautiful
buzzards, despise you, whine and bite
like deer flies. And you don't know yet
if your knees, throbbing like teeth
or conscience, are strong enough
to bear you up this dry path one more time.

Dog Kennings

Blind-born, the lucky among us
live to open round skull-windows
on light and milk; the blessed,
in domestication's fallen world,
live to share the halls of those who, among
all the legions of the furless, leave
our perilous trust in them unshattered.
Fortunate the house-hound whose upright
primate hall-fellow chooses to be kibble-giver,
bone-bearer, flea-scourger, ear-scratcher,
couch-sharer, wide-walker,
thunder-comforter; wretched the wolf
given over to the collar-twister, rib-
kicker, ignorer of empty water bowls
and frantic pleas, long-leaver,
abandoner on roads, terrible tyrant of chain.
Cursed be those torturers, cursed to wander
lonely on exile's empty road, pierced
by winter's spears, devoured alive
by the hunger so savage it drives the stray
to snatch at rotten compost where she shivers
in the slashing sleet. May heartworms
starve upon their souls' black ice.
But let heaven's hearthrug lie thick and warm
for those who, as our decade-road draws to its dead
end, offer their last guest-gift—the needle-
wielders, the givers of good sleep,
the anguish-enders, openers of the cage.

One Cup

Immortal grail of garbage,
this Styrofoam coffee cup
reels its slow way
toward the Pacific's
swirling tidal gyre
of trash four thousand miles
away, vaster than Texas,
pelagic vortex of waste
and shame; holds in its pearl
hollow the rattle of albatross
tangled in plastic line,
the bubble and sough of the great
rollers rocking their way
east before those endless
winds, till the spiral slows
them and lowers them
down; offers brief
sweet energy and heat,
dissolved in bitterness
dark as sleep and longer
than four thousand miles.

Woolly Adelgid

When the big winds boomed and
roared from peak to ridge,
the balsams bore them like anchored sloops
or wherries, broad in root
and beam, single tall masts
unseen in the strain
of the rushing black sails set full.
Whole mountainsides, those deep
battering nights, leaned and bent
and groaned in those winds,
fir needles flung like spray.

There's always a worm in the hold.
Usually it's tiny, nothing you'd think
could ever unstep the tall sails,
sink those vast fleets.
These are white as foam
frost for Christmas trees.
Like the shipworm they've gnawed
home to a haunted shell. Sails rotted
away, the masts show now,
forests of bare poles, ghost
fleets leaning over streams clear
as acid, too shallow for any keel.

After the Colony Collapse, Cullowhee, North Carolina

Oft him anhaga
are gebideð,
metudes miltse,
þeah þe he modcearig
geond lagulade . . .
wadan wræclastas.
—"The Wanderer"

The tiered square-cornered towers
are bone-cold. Barren of the bustle
and thrum of its people, our humming palace
stands hollow and still.
Where are the women, gathered together
to comb the children, balancing burnished
orange pollen pressed into panniers,
fanning nectar of frost aster
and blackberry bloom into strong sweets
for winter warmth? Far-flown,
exiles and refugees on the endless roads
of the sky, to sink at last, lost
and confused. How quickly they
fled the floors of wax and wood;
how quiet, now, the queen kneels,
that peace-giver who breathed grace
and comfort up through the colony's
stacked stories. Soon she'll be shut
in a broad black earth-chest;
and though in her glory she gave life
and life and life, slave to the hive,
raised up the gleaming ranks
and soft cells of ivory larvae,
no heir in her amber chamber waits
to wake and mate, not one daughter.
We six who stayed with her

creep or crawl our few aimless
inches, dazed with misfortune, too dismayed
even to strike at the shocked keeper—
and we were once brave battlemaids
in August's weapon-weather, fearless
foragers, tender foster-mothers.
Who will remember now the rotating
cluster, its seats at the feast?
or the dance in the dim entry, summoning
sisters to glean the sourwood gold
of summer, bear it bright
to six-sided cups in warm combs
that throbbed with song? Griefs grow
countless as white clover as we whisper
the name-scents of nurslings and sisters.
If this world's foundation is not all waste,
how shall we know? Where shall
the last of legions, left solitary,
find grace for herself, or her queen?
—Keeper, do even you know
what brought our bright rooms to ruin
and slips us into the sleep of the sting,
what pillaged the pillared honey-halls
and made mad our strong sisters,
leaving only the drumming
of the north wind's needles on the steel
ceiling that shields silent halls
haunted by hive-beetles? It is true,
after all, what the old told us,
that at last all happiness
flows cold, all this world's
stores of sweetness are fleeting and brief.

Our Lady of the Bagels

We don't know where she comes from.
Are ashamed to ask:
who over fifty chooses to stand
eight hours, ten, slicing bagels,
scraping spread? Serving, serving,
dispensing the bread of life:
our lady of the bagels, Carlleen.
I take bread and cheese
from her hard hands,
or maybe straight from her mouth,
tugged out along with silk shirts
and silver forks and decades
of education, a magician
for whom there is no end to the tricks
or the riches, whose weary assistant
lives on tips. What'll it be,
she says. Sesame seed grown
in the home of the oldest gods.
Asiago cheese flown across continents.
Wrinkled raisins and cinnamon bark.
I want Everything, I say,
give me Everything,
and with no other word, she does.

Late to the Party

It's not much of a party,
though some of the people are beautiful,
their songs throbbing deeper than rivers,
their door-grate scrolled with an iron tree
of life. Few really want to go
to the party of outrage, all that ugly
knowledge baked into the crackers
like arsenic, dissolved in the water
like lead. It's been going on
five hundred years, or ten
thousand; everyone's tired.
The toilets are all stopped up.
The crowd surges thick as blades
of dying grass; a fire of chairs reeks
and smokes on the bathroom floor
where a uniformed man clutches
himself in his arms, choking
back whimpers. Stacked against
the walls are half-sized coffins.
One woman, her ankles fluid-puffed
and veins blazing in her eyes,
holds another, who is weeping
softly with exhaustion. Like two
great trees propping each other up, black
walnuts, tulip poplars, they keep
standing: no place to sit down.
We are late to the party and reap
cynical glances: only now?
Madison makes remarks
about how things are done here,
the crack on the kitchen table, no
Pinot Grigio, slits her eyes
at a teenaged boy shrieking curses out

25

the splintered window. Tiffany whispers
that she doesn't feel very welcome,
while a tattooed girl with a rope
burn on her neck rolls a black eye.
I think that despite my outrage, myself,
I could really stand a night off,
watch CSI Special Victims—this isn't
the only party in this burning
city, not for us, not yet. When we leave,
swearing we'll be back tomorrow,
no one follows; this is where they live.

After the End

Suppose someone young, maybe someone sick
in bed, asks about us. *Crazy*
Aunt, what was it like, when clear water poured
from the walls, when couches flew
on wheels of oil, when one switch lighted
full streets? what was it like to stand on a field
made of stone, power engines
with dinosaurs, use a ton of metal
to carry two hundred pounds?

Hot, I will think but not say. *That part was mostly hot.*

And when she adds *and those sweet*
tangerines from a-whole-nother continent, wasn't
that amazing? and didn't you love seeing
bees? wasn't everyone happy? . . .
I will nod. I will speak

what she needs to hear. *Yes, I will say.*
If we cooked the world for our ease,
the feast was sweet. We didn't complain
when the power went out for an hour,
take it for granted, bicker and blame,
waste our short days seeking people to hate.
We blessed and treasured every second,
we always cherished the bees.

River of Anguish

Seeing the other side can take years, or forever.
That river runs through every town,
under every cellar. Greatest of the world's
rivers, it dwarfs the Amazon, the Yangtze,
the Paraná with its ravenous fish.
Nothing to do with it but sail it,
bridge it, choke it down, though when we drink
that brack too deep we die, too slowly.
All the ideas and adaptations—
hip boots, words, Phillips-head screws—
are bridges or spars, ferries or pumps,
crossing and harnessing anguish,
sailing close-hauled to its bonefile winds,
slowing for a moment the rivets' seep
of its corroding salts.
No one wants to swim here,
let alone drown. We all hope to wade
only to our knees, only as deep
as we can bear, even though
we know. Meanwhile,
sink the massive piles
as divers writhe with the bends;
flog horses' lathered backs
to draw the great cables taut;
as the sailors' teeth loosen with scurvy,
come about on the starboard tack.
Meanwhile, bail, oh, bail.

The Rapture

It counts as rapture only if it's quick, only
if it's not ours. Dead streams, choked children,
lesions, worms, even that skyflash
the blind could see, that's just more
of the same. No: I want a meteor,
a big one, rupturing earth out of its crust
like a baseball. Maybe a comet,
skipping its blazing tail over endless rivers
of rubble. Or a solar flare,
returning the sewers and streets,
power plants and phones and pheromones
to starry atoms, a crackle and a glare like,
guess what, the end of the world.
And I need it to have been coming
almost forever, to have begun
its trip when Lucy Australopithecus
bashed stones with stones. Then what
if we sewered and dammed the creeks, bred
and abandoned ten million dogs
or three billion people, flogged
kids for chocolate bars, hung out
our warriors like polyester laundry, then what
about Bachman's sparrow and the passenger
pigeon? No saving any of them,
no matter what we did. And, too, no more dolphins
in cages, dams locking salmon
into salt, bonecold cells with pincers and drowning
buckets, streets swallowing creeks,
the whole torturestory
forgotten forever, and if water
and warmth go too, bugleweeds and holding
hands and all the coruscating
words, well. Still. Then

it wouldn't be so bad; then we
wouldn't be so bad. We could open
our arms to the scorching hail, amputated
free like a gangrenous hand, absolved,
as if the universe shrugged, *whatever,*
game over, you're forgiven
already! It could be close as we get
to believing in heaven again, our scripture of fire
and forgiveness, it could be (almost) rapture.

Hot Flash

You had always been lucky,
tiptoeing over red
coals unblistered, just missing
the lick of flame, the terrible
shriek of the nerve;
it couldn't last forever.
You were always a witch,
which is to say a woman
not yet cowed enough,
and it couldn't be allowed.
You had to learn. They were
always going to come
for you, and find you
in the end. You were
always going to burn.

Volta

The best places are always the edges,
verges: forest becoming field,
soybean segueing into trickling
ditch. The edges are rich
with seeds, prickles, ferns,
a hundred goldenrod
species, velvet-beaded,
hedges of dotted
light and fledging wrens.

                    And here
we stand at two seasons' edge,
summer's long sea lapping
fall's packed sand, at this turn
like the turn of the tide—the utter
flood, the dead low—everything
about to flow back the other way, but not
yet. From the pause's flat sands
we gather what we can: black
shark teeth swept up
in a churn of surf. Basil's celadon
and purple opal. Morning glories, each
cerulean throat spreading its five-
point star, each a witch
glory twining its pagan spirals
and stars up crosses
and clothesline poles. Moon
snails tossed up from the tropics
of summer. We gather in what we can,
in the turn between thunder and sleet,
the pause before the wet
black road grows slick with spotted leaves,
before the cold foam ridges soak our hems.

What I Came Back For

I left that sagging house, its louring
ceilings, disapproving clocks, tight spiral
arteries of covetous love.
I swore: never again the closed
atria, the terrible hoarders'
clutter, the nerves poised to ring
with anguish like harpstrings
or crystal punch cups. No more waking
to despair in that airless room—
and yet. The rain on the outhouse roof,
gleaming on the summer ivy. An atheist
calling photosynthesis a miracle,
a woman saying *meet me*
by the sturgeons. The years we began
to guess the vast invisible
fields and reaches of gut
microbes were not in us, but were
us, those first glimmers of a stranger
family. The slow forgetting
who I am, or was, after three days
without you. I remembered. Even
out in the blessed quiet and cold,
the star-pricked black, the cauldron's slow
popple and boil, with the deadly
wheel spinning away behind, helpless
to crush me now, I shivered
to the pluck of that wire, chanced
a glance past my vanished
collarbone, picked up
one clear cup just to hand it
to someone athirst, and was lost

or (of course it's always
possible) found. Here
I am again, come back
one more time, one
more time, oh, just one more time.

The Wheel

After the five-foot wheel springs from the air,
(that is, from some truck's loosened load),
slashes like a scythe through radiator and grill,
scourging you through three lanes of charging
traffic; after you cross two seconds
in front of the semi that would have gored
and tossed you like a bull, or dragged you under
the tearing tires, or smashed you to pipes and pulp;
and after you draw your bleeding car to a pause
on the shoulder, that invisible and shuddering
shelter made only of fortune—after that,
you'd think that wheel—hubcap for some vast engine
of war? valve handle for the floodgate of the Grand Coulee?
—might stop. After all, *you've* stopped: stopped
remembering all you have to do, all the ways
you've failed; stopped forgetting to notice the hot tang
of the summer weeds bending and beating in the wind
of what spared you this time. But the wheel,
which ought to tremble, pause, and clatter
flat to rest: the wheel is still rolling. It passes
before you, where you've clambered out panting.
It crosses the shoulder, dips into the ditch and up
again, up the long bank, vaulting the barbwire fence
into the Shenandoah pasture. It passes the paused
cows, at least for now; their bemused faces say
they don't know it'll be back for them as it will
for you, and sooner. It splashes up glass fans
from the little branch, scatters shoals of minnows, and—
CEO's and senators clutching high spokes, the wretched
crushed and screaming with every revolution—
it rolls on, over hilltop, straight into horizon,
and in its wake for a moment it all falls still,
everything's calm. The throbbing asphalt sparkles

with mica, the common goldenrod glows
like copal as it all pauses, acknowledging
with a shrug and a nod your gratitude
and awe, here where you stand
alive, amazed, waiting for strangers' aid.

Seining the Parking Lot

Greensboro, Maryland

After rushing rains, the long arch of bridge
leans from land to water, and the parking
lot which is also the fairground lifts its
skeletal Ferris wheel from a hip-deep
lake; river current plunges through before
eddying and purling back to the deep
channel, carrying bright perch, smooth pewter
eels, the bones of the drowned. Down in that lake:
two people joined by thirty feet of seine,
tiny squares of net slung between two poles,
fishing for brown-gold carp—their great
opercular plates, their planks of sweet meat
to smoke pink as salmon in an oil drum
hung over a day-long sassafras fire.
No carp have swum in with the torrent, but
everything else comes up as the net's folds
and curtains sieve through the scurrying grass
shrimp, transparent as animate water:
silversides that quiver and flash and flee;
beer cans' jagged, innocent tin razors;
roseate grains of barnacles clamped by
their calcium foreheads to the glassy
elvers of the Chesapeake sea serpent;
and condoms, rinsed of any freight of joy
or shame, split now to admit passage of
squirming fingerling mermaids, or a glittering
lively handful of what, at first, could well
be bioluminescent copepods,
but which, seen close, reveal themselves to be
the sparkling larvae of the nearest stars.

Walking Home at Night, with Sonda

The glittering sprawl of the drinking gourd
stands tall on its handle, dipping
the firth of night. High
in the sky's cold clearing, its bowl
points north, toward that dim
gleam around which all stars swing.
In the black we walk
up the long dirt lane to a door
lit like a hearth. You stumble.
Then I do. You laugh, say
Don't tell me you can find your way
in this! But we do. The ground
appears as our eyes change
for a night unstained by streetlights,
flashlights, any light
save that wide sky, and that warm
small shine, faint as the little star
in the northern corner. I could find
my way here from anywhere:
true north, polestar
like that overhead, the one that led
slaves on their faring forth
to peril and terror, the lore
they'd been bred to forget.
They were your kin, as these
ahead are mine, and we
won't forget either, not yet.
The dipper quivers; the pole stands
still in the sky, as under their long arc
we walk north, toward the door.

February Sunday Noon

After the climb to the four-way crossroads
over the buried culvert's rushing creek,
I fold down onto a patch of gravel and wild onion,
wait for kinglets. Uphill, someone's deep-
voiced long-throated wind-chime strikes the air
like an hour. Chickadee, goldfinch, titmouse,
junco come and go, offering suggestions
I can't understand, reproaches I can.
The sand and pebbles of the road are still clean
from the last rain, and how the quartz and the mica
shine, the gravel of the mountain's crushed
and plundered heart accepting sunlight
with the same vast patience it brought to granite
millennia of night. The watch which maybe
I forgot to wind moves slower, slower,
each minute broader than the one before
until each could hold whole chapters.
When the kinglet comes, winter sun clear
through its tiny wings, it gives me every chance,
but, unready, I miss it time and again,
so instead I just sit: on the earth,
under the sun, the creek rustling and bubbling behind,
the chilly air stirring as if the mountain above
breathed, quivering with the echo of bells.

Mortal Minerals

It's a rainy night in April;
before the thunder came the year's
first wood thrush, a young
one, half-croaking as he tried out
his marvelous syrinx. Before that,
the tree frog, forecasting. The steady rain
is a slow rushing past the window,
hard on asphalt, soft
on dirt: tomorrow, ordinary
blessing, there'll be no need to call
on the well to quench the potato patch.
In one fine mesh of the screen a tiny drop
of rain slows the lamplight
that springs from the dirty burn
of carbon, the stored fire
of the local star: and that drop gleams
like a moth's eye.
Through the screen and the drop come
the cool scents of water, earth,
clove pinks, April
all over again, piercingly
sweet: I'd say unearthly
sweet, except that it is
earthly, entirely earthly, these are
the sweets of earth, this
is us, mortal minerals
in the brief era of stars, this is it.

Luna

A mouse has gnawed the dead luna moth,
leaving only the veined celadon sails
made to cross the black lakes of these few nights—
devouring sailor and ship, and the pale shores
of evening, and even the crescent's spring-green
sickle, so that tonight, if you meet it,
you'll know which mouse it was:
the one whose silver ears trim and turn
to catch the May wind, the one who shines like the moon.

Snail Kite, Okeechobee

The red-tailed hawk's antithesis,
this soot-gray kite with white-barred tail,
hunter of marshes, nemesis
of uncombative apple snails,
has no such flexibility;
it eats only the escargots
it orders, with an agility
hard to believe, seen from below,
with gripping talon, and a beak
that's grown to fit the snail's shell—
that shell alone—in an oblique
curve like the sound bow of a bell
that speaks its note each time, just right;
each time it strikes that one, no other.
The niche-perfected snail kite
can't trim its vanes to fit the weather,
change to a more useful trick
when apple snails run out, or start
a new career. Its fantastic
skill is all it has, one art
of picking out just what it needs
from a buffet that has no use
at all, save snails. So it feeds
while they continue, pecks and chooses,
a hunger artist of the shallow
grassy waters, glinting veins
of sky and cat's-paw dapples, mallows,
bright reaches of reflected sun:
hieratic, specialized, arcane,
bound to its dwindling domain,
subsisting on its one thing, one.

Hornets' Nest

Gray paper sack full of venom:
you've watched its dark door since the last
blackberry brambles loosed their grip
on jagged crimson leaves rimed with
silver, revealing the soft nest
suspended from a slender bar
of lightweight hooks and needles.
Now, though, when you come
with clippers, bear it home to hang
in triumph from your ceiling,
it looks different now. Swollen large
as a cow's heart, ringed with barbwire
thorns, it pulses gravity like
some clouded moon, the blind black hole
at the bottom a wordless mouth.
First the earth, then its glittering
chain of satellite trash begins
to realign, to circle around
this homemade house, this labyrinth
of women, of makers, one of
the endless ominous softly
throbbing hearts of everything.

Day of the Dead

It's the second of the year's two Days
of the Dead. Your marigolds
froze; you never got around to shaping sugar
skulls, or dead-bread, but you're raking
the hill road, even though you love the fallen
leaves, because you loathe the blare
of your neighbor's blower, and because it's gentle
exercise for the shoulder you tore trying to roll
a kayak which had no plans to go anywhere
but over. The westerly breeze rises,
and the sun leans through that cold roll
of cloud over the far ridge, and suddenly
it's leaves, leaves everywhere, turning
and turning, sifting, spinning, sailing.
The whole shining height of the air
fills with them, innumerable as shaken grains
of salt: oak, poplar, cherry, poison
ivy, even a few from the stripling
American chestnuts still starring this hill,
too young yet for the blight. They blow between
porch boards, and into the lee of every rotting log,
and onto the road you're raking, making
you wonder about this use of your time.
Every current, every level of air is brief
harbor for a goldfinch leaf, the way it was
when you were a kid, outside for this instead
of at your desk. The sun pours through
the leaves, and turns the dun wall
of the neighbor's house briefly white.
And you're forty-six, and your parents are seventy-
five, still strong, still clear. You can walk;
you have all your fingers, gripping
the rake. Rain has filled the well. The woods
are bright with the sweet-betsy bushes

and the tawny hickories offering back
the light they drank all year,
and the leaves are flying like spirits
as you rake the blessed road.
Like the crazy old woman
you're slowly becoming, you say aloud
to the road, *I can never forget this,*
by which, of course, you mean you'll never remember.

Ways to Talk about Decay

Gone bad, we say, as if milk were an apple-
faced innocent fallen into rough
company, smoking the wrong
bacteria, hardening like cider;
as if the loyal, patriotic Longhorn
had tasted blood, bedecked itself
with mold-pocks and become
a deadly man-eating cheese. *Gone
over,* we say, as if there's a line in graveyard
loam, this side, that side, and last week's smoke-
steeped chicken stepped over: now
it's a plat-eye, guarding its cursed
treasure, hoarding harm, wanting
you to come over too. Or *turned,*
we say, as if orange juice's bright sting,
which you took for a friend or at least
a forgiving slave, has finally remembered
what it used to be—an ovary
for generations, a thick, wedding-
sweet blossom, whose child you took
 to be pulped and crushed—so now it's turned
its back on you. And then *turned,*
we say, as if the butter has turned
like the meander of a river, taken that sour
curve it's yearned for ever since the churn.
As if you and the milk were walking together
on a dirt road whose berm you thought
ran clear to the illusion of horizon,
but suddenly the sun has slipped,
the air forewarned evening chill,
the downhill ruts and gouges grown
a worm-curl bend. There could be anything
twenty feet on, fireflies, prehistoric ferns,

tall stones, and now the milk
in its carton has gone on ahead;
it's already out of sight of where you stand
baffled, betrayed, alone on that torn road
in the autumn twilight. There's no returning,
and you don't want to follow, oh, no,
but for a moment you can't discern
just what to do. And over its curved
shoulder the milk didn't spare you a look
before it went that way, before it turned.

Stripping

You're not willing yet. Maybe you tried skinny-dipping,
came up with leeches, and that wasn't the undressing
earth wanted anyway. So the skin's
a little spotted, but silky and warm,
and still so pretty. So the joints throb
in the rain, or the bones pop, is that any cause
to just call up Goodwill, give them away?
But you will; you'll get naked,
pare down like an old stripper taking her final
show, the crowd lukewarm. Tender
fat will roll off like a wet sweater; some beetle will cut
loose those tendons, easing the strain they've borne
so long. Soon it will feel inevitable, right,
relief like peeling off stockings and wire-bound
bra after fifteen hours, falling into night.
Even the rib cage will seem too tight,
constricting those feral parts, but the cage
will open now, the soft organs' hour
is here. At the last the heart shakes
the settling bones, mad to be off,
the liver's black lobes are frantically trembling,
the dark little gall bladder is almost free
from its bitter career. Even the slippery
gray brain can tell it's about to be out
on its own, no more bone helmets, touched
by everything, opened into the equally
spongy, desirous, bare-naked world.

The Young

for the new teachers

The young need the old.
You wouldn't think it, to see
them toss their hair silky as the ears
of vampire bats, their eyes focused on nothing
you can see. You wouldn't think it
from the sound of the giggling
almost too high to hear, offering you less
notice than the cries of hunting
bats. But the young
need you. They need your
time, your ear for their keening
and chiming, even when it means nothing
you know. Your admiration
and pity for their brashness
and tenderness, your abnegation
of what you hoped to do this hour,
which for either of you comes once
only. Your approval, for the like of which
many an adult still goes thirsty, fifty
years on. Your life drained out to feed
their unfocused need. They drink
it like bats too, eternally beautiful for having
bathed in your blood like Bathory
countesses. They do it helplessly,
as you do to your own beloved old,
who forgive you, helplessly
as you'll forgive these, as the weakening
cow forgives the hungry bat,
its dainty fangs, its fingers for wings.

Chickweed, Hens

The chickweed in its loose lush
viridian sprawl hurls out
arms and spokes, wheels reeling from
heart-hubs into green galaxies
of spear-heart leaves, spattered with
speckled stars—all light-spawned
themselves from the nearby star,
this one sun. To eat of this
opportunistic shallow-
root, this transfigured sunlight,
you must grasp the center;
you must take it by the heart,
then bear its pulsing spirals
to hungry hens whose harsh beaks
peck it apart, snap it down,
gulp up tiny lives riding
its long sprays and spurs, devour
the vivid freshness of spring-
greens to reverse those spinning wheels,
turn those armed clocks back to sun-
orange, yolk-gold, fat food: the
other transfiguration,
this work of winged, warm-blooded
reptiles, the savage women
of summer, the layers of life.

Womb-room

You always pictured it black in there, if less black
like a windowless underground cell than black
as an iris, a silky queen-of-night tulip, why not—
what the speculum saw, stabbing its annual spear
of light, you never did, that room had neither sun
nor sea nor even the blood-tide moon.
Only now there's the screen, its mystic
mirror promising terrible truths. Now,
now, here's all you never thought to see—
and it's not black. No tulip-cup, no sealed cell,
but a witch-cathedral of rose quartz, peony petals,
arched, vaulted, glimmering with moisture like the geode
walls of hidden caverns at the first candlelight
in that deep underground. Made to hold a life
it couldn't hold, still this could be a secret chamber
of Luray, Fingal, Lascaux, this room
inside yourself into which you could almost step,
whose curved walls you could almost inscribe
with ochre does, cows, mares, wild
cats, new countries, charts of unnamed stars.

The Lycanthrope

When the last full moon of autumn pulls
just below the rim of the sky,
when the world begins to roll
into its radiance like a dog into sun,
scalp-hair and arm-hair stir, ruffle as if
in the wind of a comet's tail,
and the woman at the window lays down
her spatula and knife, turns to the half
open door, crosses the whispering
leaves and flat dirt as dusk eats
the last colors, into the woods
where she sinks to the gray ground,
kicks off shoes, struggles
first out of jeans and then out of face
and fingers, into muzzle and paw,
hackle and fang, a tail that tells no lies.

It's supposed to end with savaged
chickens, ropes of bowel, shotguns
and a clamor of hounds, that old bad story.
But the truth is that she lives
largely on mice, though she won't refuse a teacup
poodle. Tonight she snaps up
a late squirrel, breaks its neck
with her trademark shake, takes it in her jaws
where she is going: to the den
in the umber clay of a gully bank.
There she rests in the mouth of the earth
as the moon climbs the scales of cloud:
crunches the spine, gnaws the skull,
savors the entrails, nibbles the bony tail.
She is only coyote now, returning
where the wolves were driven out:

stealthier, lower, less glamor,
more craft. When she is poisoned or shot,
there'll be others, shadows, sisters
and nieces, all yellow-tan, scrawny, brush-tailed.
The squirrel is small, but sustains her for now.
The men with the guns don't know where she is,
much less how this happened: that there was never
a monster, an infection, a terrible change.
No one bit her. She's always been this way.

After Anguish

God, I say in anguish, god,
make it stop. But if you invoke
gods, you have to go out in the dirt
where they work, so I draw on a man's shirt
and set to mowing the gods' and the bees'
sweet clover, the plantains which heal
boils and wounds, all the tangle
of blameless yard grass, until I have mown down
some of my fury and shame—though soon,
no doubt, they'll be back. Afterwards,
from where I've dropped
into the hammock, momentarily calm,
I see where yellowjackets have dug a nest
in the nearby clay: if I'd cut a foot
closer, this day would have ended worse.
As it is, the wasps and I were spared
for this brief peace. The coming fall's puffballs
are forming their dirt-stars in the dry July
grass. Not angry, not fearful,
though by December they'll be dead,
the yellowjackets pass in and out of their door
searching last year's leaves for what—
paper for soft walls? prey
for their young?—may make their house
sweeter, or warmer, or safer
against despair. I will go in now
to my house, and bring them a spoonful of jam.

Billy Collins Pours Me a Beer

Sarah Lawrence College, Summer 2001

First came the writers' softball game,
the lithe and the clumsy hustling and scrambling
together in green June heat, the gangly
man on second, Billy something. I was deep
in right field, safe from falling
balls, reading the grass for carrion
daisies and lucky leaves of clover,
until someone yelled *run,*
you poet laureate! Oh. *That* Billy.

Afterwards I met him at the station
of the keg, where he drew me a plastic cup
of pointed silver bubbles in modest
domestic amber. *I have to say something,* I thought,
slightly dazed, like someone grazed
by a softball. *I have to sound smart.*
Nothing. No *nice lanyard,* no *Baudelaire*
calls me his brother. All those words,
and I found only two, though I think now,

if I had to choose, there are worse words
than those we offer bartenders for scotch,
heaven for unearned grace, or Mary Watkins
who cleans the office for her long labor
with the heavy mop, for the brief order
she drags out of all that star litter's
primal cruelty and decay, over and over,
one more time, one more day. *Thank you,*
I said, turning away, like I hadn't heard,
like I didn't know, like I'd never read a word.

Fairy Tale

What if hope weren't a treacherous ghost
of all you'd lost, always
drawing away at the exact pace
of your desperate forward crawl? what
if better were ever coming, if there were
someone to help lug the feet
of the corpse you have to drag
and drag by its softening armpits
—and all you had to do was hold off
quitting or killing yourself another few
days, another few years?
 if you found yourself
with time to paddle bright
rivers, and your kayak roll was all right—
not perfect, but enough to heave you upright
again, to save you from drowning?

Forget seeing the beloved dead again
in some ragged orchard of long autumn
grass, sassafras berries dropping
blueblack from their scarlet cups, the fallen
oaks unfelling themselves, your river
fit to drink again, the lost freshwater
mussels creeping back
home, each on its one slow foot.
Forget being absolved
or forgotten by the people
you once hurt, forget ever seeing
him again, no one's talking
about heaven. I'm talking about what if
your dreams weren't always
bad: would you know what to do
with them? what if
it turned out you were nearly good
enough after all?

Squash Vine

From the fermenting mash by the shed
come bristly, twisty stems, hairy and fibrous,
noose-twining vines, thirsty
roots, wordless gourd-leaves reaching,
stretching to the size of hands, then dinner
plates, then great umbrellas.
This cucurbit eats the compost pile, swamps
the tomatoes, threshes down
decay, makes vanish the trash
and mush of skins and pits.
It may yet be smitten with worms,
but today it is green on the earth, today
it is exceedingly glad in its rush
to produce ruffle-edged fruit
white as scalloped moons, improbable
as flying saucers: if we let it,
it could offer anyone clemency
from the hammers of the sun, or the blaze
of our endless mistakes, if we let it
it could shade the whole world.

Night Driving, Lighted Windows

Despite all the night terrors, despite
the knotted fists and brutal words,
toilets and trash cans running over,
chained dogs, the reek of meth
or whiskey, fabric softener or vomit,
every lamplit window glows gold
as every other—no matter what's gone
on inside, or is still going.
And each white shed-fluorescent speaks
of workbenches, oiled chisels,
screwdrivers, someone shaping
a shelf or rewiring a washer,
making, mending. Passing
those calm yellow squares,
I can almost believe
in someone quietly handing coffee,
a towel, a deep cup of soup,
and someone else glancing up: *thanks.*
I can almost believe
that if someone lost came
tapping at that window,
the bolt would fly back in welcome.
Those windows' warm gleams
shine out for miles, telling their
beautiful stories, some of them
maybe true.
                        —And I, on my way home,
plunging into my brief funnel of light,
I fly past like a witch on the gale,
soothing down fear, smoothing
wrath with my passage: my invisible
gaze remaking the world
for a moment into that place where even now

we are all warm and have enough
inside our square stars, we are
forgiving those who share
the world with us, choosing
to be kind, making
and mending what we can.

Spouse, Assembling Honey Frames

I can keep, or fail to keep, the honeybees. Can bring them
water, fresh frames to hold the freight
of nectar, condensed and fanned to heavy honey.
Can bear them sugar, re-stack them after storm.
Can wade into the hum of the swarm to make
a desperate split, to keep the bees home. Can
mourn them when they weaken, when they die,
can bite back panic when they pierce the veil,
can take the hot hair-wire of the sting,
the sick shiver of the spreading venom.

But I can't build. Power tools stalk me with death
in their red eyes, saws cant their paired teeth
up toward my foot, nails twist awry. It's he,
who never wanted bees, who builds the hives,
the boxes with their corners clean and square,
the lightwood frames around the slender screens
of wax foundation, wax the bees will shape
into cells and fill with honey, a drop
for every ten thousand blooms stroked
and ravished, almost too sweet to bear.

He does what he always has: checks
the details, trues up the ends, fits the pins
and staples, drives the tacks, secures
the fragile frames made to store blackberry
blossom, ephemeral clover, the sticky syrup
of tulip poplar, sourwood's buttery gold—
summer's distillation of the marriage
of bee and nectary, performed anew each time
in endlessly repeated celebration—
to hold the great, astounding weight
of all earth's mortal sweetness. And they will.

The Promise

Life-root, blazing out in your golden rags.
Killdeer, skimming the soccer field,
pealing the glad word of May. Soft lamb's
quarter, powdered with pewter dust
that might've come from the Horsehead
Nebula, putting spinach to shame
with your mineral riches. Wood
thrush trilling your deep flute-
notes from the high canopy, almost never
seen. Tiny henbit, more glamorous
and sexy in your freckled orchid pink
than Marilyn Monroe's . . . et cetera.
Et cetera. The list goes on longer
and deeper than any human voice,
and how many hear any of you
over the clamor of ad and ego,
how many know you were ever
here? Nor can I save you
when they come with the mowers,
the poisons, nor regrow rainforests
for thrushes, nor make the world
plant milkweed for its true-born monarchs.
I can do only what I am
doing: look for you. Listen
as you proclaim your endless
names in all the tongues
of earth. Tell those names back:
as long as lichens
star this mountain's boulder-bones
with flat seaglass rosettes,
so that even the rock blooms

some wordless joy
into the day's high air, I will
not cease telling. I will go on
doing my work in this world.

* 9 7 8 0 8 0 7 1 6 9 8 8 9 *